HOW
ON
EARTH
DO
WE
RECYCLE
METAL?

HOW ON EARTH DO WE RECYCLE

METAL?

BY RUDY KOUHOUPT

with

DONALD B. MARTI, JR.

Illustrations by

ART SEIDEN
and
RUDY KOUHOUPT

THE MILLBROOK PRESS
Brookfield, Connecticut

The photos are courtesy of
Steel Can Recycling Institute, pp. 13, 26;
Institute of Scrap Recycling Industries, Inc., pp. 14, 19, 23;
American Iron and Steel Institute, pp. 15, 16;
Reynolds Aluminum Recycling Co., pp. 17, 21;
City of New York, Dept. of Sanitation, p. 20;
Paul E. Phaneuf, p. 25

Produced in association with **STEARN/KNUDSEN & CO.**

Printed in the United States of America
5 4 3 2 1

Library of Congress Cataloging-in-Publication Data
Kouhoupt, Rudy, 1931-.
How on earth do we recycle metal? / by Rudy Kouhoupt with Don Marti;
illustrated by Art Seiden.
p. cm.
Includes bibliographical references and index.
Summary: Examines the problems associated with the disposal of metal waste
and describes how it can be recycled by creating objects such as jewelry,
weather vanes, and Christmas ornaments.

ISBN 1-56294-142-9

1. Metal wastes — Recycling — Juvenile literature. 2. Metal work — Juvenile
literature . [1. Metal wastes — Recycling. 2. Recycling (Waste) 3. Metalwork.
4. Handicraft.] I. Marti, Don, 1968- . II. Seiden, Art, ill. III. Title.
TD799.5.K68 1992
669—dc20
91-28953 CIP AC

This book is printed on recycled paper.

CONTENTS

Egyptian gold-smiths create golden vases in this fresco from around the 15th century B.C.

1 HOW ON EARTH DO WE RECYCLE METAL?

Turning Swords Into Plowshares

Precious metals, such as gold, silver, and platinum, are so valuable that no one ever thinks of throwing them away. No matter how many times metal is melted down and turned into something else, it remains just as good as new.

Recycling may sound like a modern-day invention, but ever since people first learned to use metal, they have reused it over and over again. The bronze blade of a plowshare might have been used to cut furrows in the earth for many generations. Then, when war broke out, the metal from that plowshare would be melted down and mixed with scrap bronze to form a sword. This sword would go from hand to hand until it too was melted, divided, and mixed with metals from a mine in Europe, Asia, or the Middle East.

Thousands of years later, a bit of the bronze from this sword might form a shiny medallion on a chain. One day, after the medallion has passed from generation to generation, it might end up in the scrap metal used to make the electrical wiring inside a tractor's engine—and that tractor might pull a plow.

Metals Through the Ages

Much of the earth contains metal. Metals have a luster, or shine, and they are able to conduct heat and electricity. There are over 80 kinds of metals and metal compounds. They vary considerably in hardness and in their ability to be melted, molded, and stretched. In this book we will talk about only a few of the most common ones.

In China and Egypt, gold and silver were used for ornaments, jewelry, and utensils as early as 3500 B.C. Even before written history, people discovered how to separate pure metal from rocks, or ores, in a process called smelting. Copper, which was found both in a pure form and in ore, was the most widely used metal in these early times.

Egyptian metalworkers smelted copper inside a clay furnace the size of a garbage can. A wood fire heated the ore until it turned into a liquid, and when the fire cooled, pure copper was left at the bottom of the furnace. While it was still soft, they molded it into any number of useful or beautiful objects.

Soon after the discovery of copper smelting, people invented a new metal alloy, or mixture of metals. Perhaps someone put tin ore into a smelting oven by mistake along with the copper ore. What a pleasant surprise to find that this metal was harder and stronger than either copper or tin by itself! This shiny new alloy was called bronze.

The widespread use of bronze gave its name to the period of time known as the Bronze Age. Many of the events in the Bible's Old Testament and much of the history of ancient Greece and Egypt took place during the Bronze Age.

People around the world melted and shaped metals as the Egyptians had. Because they had to make them by hand, metals were very valuable. Metal tools and weapons were fixed and resharpened many times or melted down and reshaped. Archaeologists have found almost no metal tools in ancient garbage heaps!

In Egypt, though, they have dug many metal objects from tombs. The Egyptians placed precious possessions alongside their dead pharoahs, whom they buried in enormous tombs known as pyramids. They believed that the tools, weapons, and ornaments would be used by the dead in the afterlife.

Whether or not the ancient Egyptians found life after death, many of their metal belongings did: grave robbers often dug them out and recycled them! Much later, archaeologists unearthed these fascinating objects—from those tombs that had escaped the robbers—and they are now in museums for everyone to see.

Iron and Steel: Strong and Useful Metals

The metal we use most today is iron. And most of our iron is made into strong steel—an alloy of iron, carbon, and small amounts of other substances.

Iron was known during the Bronze Age, but it was difficult to mine, and blacksmiths in most countries were not able to build ovens hot enough to melt the stubborn metal. They forged iron by heating it red-hot over a charcoal fire and then beating it into shape with hammers. The result was what is called wrought iron. Only the Chinese had furnaces hot enough to melt iron, which they poured into molds, or casts, to make bells.

Between 1500 and 1200 B.C. the Bronze Age began to give way to the Iron Age, when blacksmiths in Anatolia (now Turkey) developed methods of making harder, better iron. About the same time, they discovered—perhaps by accident—that small amounts of carbon from the charcoal in the fire combined with the iron to form steel.

Around 500 B.C., Indian metalworkers discovered a way to make liquid iron into an even tougher, higher-quality steel, but they kept their technique a secret. By the seventh century A.D., Arab metalsmiths had learned how to apply the Indian techniques. Apparently, these were almost completely forgotten after the Islamic empire disintegrated in the tenth century.

Ironworking skills changed little in the Western world until the invention of firearms in the fourteenth century. Swords and armor could be made of wrought iron, but the best way of making the large cannons used in battle was to cast them.

The difficulty of melting iron for casting was solved by the invention of the blast furnace. The first one was built in Massevaux, France, in 1409. Leather bellows pumped blasts of air into a charcoal fire. Church bells and cannons were cast at Massevaux. Soon more blast furnaces were built elsewhere in France, as well as in Britain, Belgium, and Germany.

During the late 1600s, iron manufacturing was a big business in England. But there was a problem: charcoal was the only fuel that burned hot enough to melt iron, and it was made from wood, which meant the English had to cut down many of their trees. As a result, the price of charcoal shot up and production slowed down.

Metal smelting in Europe, 1683.

Abraham Darby, a partner in a brass wire company, got the idea of making cooking pots from cast iron, but he needed to find a more economical fuel than charcoal. Coal was heavily mined in England and used in glassmaking and smelting copper, tin, and lead. Coal was unsuitable for ironmaking, though. It had too many contaminants and clogged the furnaces. As a young apprentice, Darby had visited breweries, and he remembered that in brewing beer, malt was dried in ovens that used a fuel called coke, made from coal. In 1709, he successfully experimented with coke in his blast furnace at

Coalbrookdale, in the West Country. His discovery meant that England could produce more iron—and save its trees.

Other ironmakers quickly copied Darby. Because England had an almost unlimited amount of the coal needed to make coke, it became the world's largest manufacturer of iron.

Eighteenth-century England saw many advances in mining and ironmaking, which led to the development of improved iron and brass machinery. James Watt's invention of the steam engine (1769) was one of the most important of these machines, because it was driven by a new source of energy: steam. The steam engine could run machinery continuously. For example, the textile industry could now use machines to spin yarn and weave cloth in factories, instead of relying on people working on hand-driven machinery at home. Steam engines ran machinery that greatly increased coal production, permitting iron foundries to work throughout the night. With the steam engine came the age of mass production.

This revolutionary steam engine, designed by James Watt, helped bring the world into the industrial age.

New uses for iron transformed transportation as well. Horses pulled heavy loads in wooden wagons along wooden tracks until 1767, when cast-iron wheels and tracks began to be used. This change, along with improvements in the steam engine, led to the development of the railway in the nineteenth century. In 1781, at

Coalbrookdale, a grandson of Abraham Darby completed the first cast-iron bridge.

Advances were also taking place in steelmaking. Benjamin Huntsman, a Sheffield clockmaker, opened a steel foundry to produce stronger steel springs for his clocks. In about 1740, he mixed high-quality wrought iron with charcoal in special tall clay pots, called crucibles. These pots were covered and placed in a large, coke-burning furnace. When the pots were removed from the red-hot fire and the molten (liquid) metal poured into molds, the result was superior steel. Huntsman had rediscovered the Indian method of making steel. The secret was that the carbon had to be evenly distributed throughout the molten metal. Over the years, further discoveries enabled the steel industry to make larger quantities of steel more cheaply.

Eventually, England became the leader of the Industrial Revolution, which spread throughout Europe and the United States in the last quarter of the nineteenth century. The transition from an agricultural society to an industrial one has altered our lives forever.

Canned Food, Safe Food

For many years, beginning in 1793, the French and the British were at war. But food poisoning and malnutrition were killing more French soldiers than died in battle. So France offered a prize for the first person who could invent a safe way to store food for the army and navy.

In 1810, a young Frenchman called Nicholas Appert won the prize for packing food in airtight bottles. He heated the full bottles to kill germs, then sealed them with corks.

The French troops now had a safe, convenient way to carry their food. But soon the British Army invented a better way. An Englishman, Peter Durand, made containers out of iron covered with a layer of tin, and packed food into them. The tin prevented the iron from rusting. Also, iron was lighter than glass and didn't break as easily—especially when soldiers had to march long distances. Today we call these metal containers tin cans. Modern cans are made out of steel, but they are still coated with tin.

For about 100 years, cans were made by hand. Using solder—a soft mixture of tin and lead—tinsmiths soldered pieces of metal together. Then the food was put in and the lid attached by hand.

Not many people would throw away something that took that much work to make. Old cans were turned into cups and candleholders. One nineteenth-century company made a baby powder can with a piece of metal inside. When the powder was gone, the can became a rattle for the baby!

Steel cans provide strong, safe, and convenient packaging. Americans use more than 100 million every day.

Both tin and steel are valuable metals. Steel is strong and easy to recycle, yet it can rust. Tin is soft, but a thin layer of tin protects steel from rusting. If you mix tin and steel together, however, the resulting metal is weaker than pure steel and it still rusts. Therefore, in order to recycle steel cans, the steel and the tin must be separated.

Today, detinning plants separate tin from steel by first using paint thinner to remove the paint from the cans, then dissolving the tin in a special solution. An electric current draws the tin out of the solution and deposits it on iron bars. Then the bars are heated, and the melted tin runs off.

During World War II, when the Japanese invaded many of the countries where tin is mined, the United States needed tin for its armed forces. A big recycling program for steel cans began. People were asked to turn in their old steel cans.

Young people's organizations, such as the Boy Scouts of America, collected thousands of tons of steel cans. In some towns, stores requested one used can for every canned item they sold. Other towns collected cans in separate containers on their garbage trucks. Today, communities are rediscovering the benefits of recycling metal.

Junker Cars and Scrap Metal

In our country, one major source of metal waste is cars. Although many used cars are sold to new owners, about ten million cars become junk every year. The first stop for a junker, or wrecked car, is often an auto salvage yard, or junkyard. At the salvage yard, people can buy parts from the wreck.

Some salvage-yard operators shred cars themselves; others sell them to a shredding company. According to the Institute of Scrap Recycling, in 1990 there were about 220 shredders in the United States, and they processed nine million cars.

Shredders rip automobiles into fist-sized pieces of steel in less than a minute. In 1990, the U.S. scrap recycling industry processed over nine million junked automobiles.

When the cars go into the shredder, they are chopped up into little pieces of metal, glass, and plastic. Often the only parts that are saved are the metal pieces, mostly steel. The bits of plastic and glass are buried in a landfill.

Scrap steel from shredded cars is sold to steel companies. They melt the scrap down to make new steel for cans and other steel products. It's possible that an old wreck will come back in a few months as a shiny new car!

An electromagnet carries two one-ton bales of shredded steel scrap to an oxygen furnace.

Other scrap steel comes from old buildings, ships, and railroad tracks. Factories that make products from steel usually ship their steel scrap back to the steel mill to be recycled. Business people known as scrap brokers make recycling deals: they arrange for the shipment of scrap steel from one company that wants to sell it to another that needs it to make new steel. Some scrap also comes from steel left over at the steel mill itself.

Much of the steel used in homes, however, is not recycled. Old refrigerators, stoves, pots, pans, and tools often get hauled away with the garbage instead of being taken to scrap recyclers.

But one company in New Jersey, Prolerized Schiabo Neu, not only shreds cars but buys and cuts up steel doors and beams from old buildings, desks, hot-water heaters, and shelving. It takes appliances but not motors, which sometimes contain hazardous materials. After the iron and steel is removed with a magnet, other metals are sorted by hand. The mixed materials that are left are resold.

Recycling has always been a part of the process of making steel. Whenever iron is converted into steel, the company adds some scrap. In fact, the more scrap that steel contains, the stronger it becomes. One ton of recycled steel makes as much metal as 3 1/2 tons of raw materials, and it takes 74 percent less energy to make steel from scrap than it does from ore. Recycling scrap iron and steel means less air pollution from burning fuel. It also saves millions of cubic yards of landfill.

More than half of the steel used in the United States comes from recycling. The increase in recycling has given rise to minimills, which are built specifically for steel scrap. The minimill industry produces 20 percent of the total steel output in the United States.

Aluminum Smelting

Charles Martin Hall was studying chemistry at Oberlin College in Ohio when he first heard about aluminum. He learned that the metal was strong and light and that it didn't rust. But, his teacher told him, it was almost impossible to smelt.

Aluminum ore was plentiful in many countries. Yet, making aluminum from the ore was so difficult to do that the metal, which we now take for granted, was more expensive than silver.

In 1886, when Hall was 22, he discovered a way to make aluminum by passing an electric current through the ore. He started an aluminum company, and his teacher had to change what he taught in class. Hall's company became Aluminum Company of America (ALCOA), which is now the largest aluminum manufacturer in the world.

Today, many things are made from aluminum, such as siding for houses, parts of airplanes and cars, foil, and beverage cans.

Aluminum companies still use electricity to make the metal. But with the amount of electricity needed to make one aluminum can from aluminum ore, they can recycle 20 cans. Even though two thirds of the aluminum cans in the United States are recycled, a lot still end up in the garbage. Each American uses an average of one aluminum can every day!

Many manufacturers provide buy-back centers where consumers bring cans and receive payment.

Deadly Batteries

A car battery produces electricity from a chemical reaction between lead and sulfuric acid. Lead is a soft, heavy metal that forms the plates inside the battery. Lead and acid make good batteries that can be recharged many times. Today, most lead is used to make batteries.

But lead is poisonous. At the time of the Roman Empire, some people drank wine from lead cups. Doctors think that the wine absorbed some of the lead, and that many ancient Romans may have died from lead poisoning!

To keep the lead in a car battery from polluting the water when you throw it away, some states have laws that require every mechanic to recycle an old battery when putting in a new one.

When a driver goes to an auto-parts store for a car battery, the price includes a trade-in for an old one. The stores send the old batteries to a plant where the plastic cases are cut open and the lead is melted down to make new batteries. Four-fifths of all the lead used in car batteries is recycled.

The small batteries in flashlights, tape recorders, and electronic games don't have lead in them. But some of them contain mercury or other poisonous metals.

Unlike car batteries, these other batteries usually cannot be recycled. You can cut down on waste by using rechargeable batteries or buying an adapter to let you run battery-powered devices from house current. Some towns collect small batteries in steel barrels to keep them from poisoning the water underground.

Collecting Waste: Incinerators and Landfills

Everybody throws things away. You throw away paper at school. Factories throw away truckloads of scraps left over from production. Your family throws away hundreds of things—paper and plastic wrappings, newspapers, aluminum foil, cans, broken toys, food scraps, and leaking pens. Most of what you bring into the house ends up in the garbage. Imagine how nasty your neighborhood would smell if all the garbage piled up, uncollected, outside people's houses.

More than 100 years ago, New York City smelled terrible. Besides garbage, the streets were filled with horse manure! So, New York City started the first American garbage collecting program. At first, the city used garbage scows. These ships carried garbage out to sea, where it was dumped overboard.

Scow trimmers, the first full-time recyclers, were people who boarded garbage scows and searched the garbage for valuable items. They collected clothing and metal objects to keep or sell.

Soon after garbage collecting began, several cities started the first organized recycling programs. They passed laws requiring people to sort their garbage into several categories. Paper, metal, glass, and other valuable materials were collected and sold. Food scraps went to garbage cookers, where they were boiled and dried, then sold as pig food. By World War I, 70 percent of the cities in the United States had recycling programs.

But cities halted their recycling programs as it became cheaper to bury waste than to separate and reuse it. The city sanitation departments that had been recycling waste began building incinerators and digging landfills instead. In an incinerator, garbage burns in a large oven. Sometimes the heat from the burning garbage is used to make steam. That steam can then be used in factories or to generate electricity.

Turn-of-the-century scrap-metal peddlers were the first metal recyclers in the U.S. They bought scrap, processed it, and sold it to smelters, mills and refiners.

After the federal government passed the Clean Air Act, in 1970, many incinerators had to close. That meant that more and more garbage was going to the landfills.

In a landfill, garbage is dumped in a deep hole the size of many city blocks. Earth-moving machinery is used to cover the garbage with dirt. But landfills have problems of their own. When rain passes through a landfill, it can carry poisons from the garbage into streams and underground water, known as groundwater. Landfills must be carefully tested to make sure they do not pollute lakes, streams, and wells.

Someone must take samples of the water in every landfill and test the water for pollution. If the landfill is run by a city or county, a chemist for the sanitation or health department does the testing. If the landfill is run by a private company, the company's workers do the testing.

A new landfill has to be carefully planned. It should not be too near lakes and streams; there should be good roads nearby so that trucks can bring garbage in. The landfill should be close to the city so that the trucks don't have to go far, but not too close, or the land will be too expensive. People don't want landfills near their homes. Trash blows over the fence and lands on lawns and gardens; the heavy machinery in the landfill is extremely noisy; and hundreds of garbage trucks drive past every day.

Soon many of the nation's landfills will close because people are producing too much garbage. Reducing and recycling waste is more important than ever.

With all these problems, it is hard to find places to put new landfills. Because landfill space is scarce, it is becoming expensive. In some eastern states, such as New Jersey, it costs more than $100 to dump a ton of garbage. That's 5 cents a pound. If you throw away 5 pounds a day—the national average—you're spending 25 cents a day just to get rid of your garbage.

This mountain of aluminum cans will be recycled and turned into new cans that may be back on store shelves in less than six weeks.

Communities Turn to Recycling

The high cost of landfills is the big reason why cities are turning to recycling to help get rid of their garbage. Often the value of recycled garbage isn't high enough to pay for the cost of recycling it, but savings in landfill costs can make recycling worthwhile.

People have to ask many questions when they decide whether to recycle garbage in their city. How much does it cost to throw away our garbage now? Will there be landfill space for our garbage in the future? How much will it cost to recycle garbage?

Then they have to decide whether city workers or a private company will do the recycling. Some cities use city-owned trucks to collect recyclable materials. In New York City, the Department of Sanitation picks up newspapers, glass, metal, and plastic.

Other communities have contracts with private companies. One big recycler is Waste Management, Inc., which owns many trash collection companies. Making a deal with a company saves the town's government much of the hassle of setting up a recycling program. The company takes care of details such as buying trucks and finds buyers for the materials it collects.

Find out what kind of recycling program your community has. Does your family separate garbage for recycling? Different places have different kinds of programs. One program, which collects recyclable material from every house, is called a curbside program. Other programs have drop-off points, where people can take their recyclables. Many supermarkets collect cans and bottles this way, providing a refund for a deposit received at the time of purchase.

A third kind of program uses buy-back centers, where a company pays people for their recyclable material. A lot of aluminum is recycled this way, because aluminum is valuable and easy to recycle.

Some Boy Scouts, Girl Scouts, and members of other youth organizations collect aluminum cans in parks and along roads, and then take them to the buy-back center. This doesn't just clean up the environment, it also raises money for the group.

In New York City, a young actor and writer named Guy Polhemus came up with a way to help the homeless. He started a redemption, or buy-back, center called "We Can" where poor and homeless people receive money for the cans and bottles they gather from the streets. We Can has developed into a small industry and now works with United Parcel Service to collect recyclable drink containers from businesses, residences, schools, and religious organizations. The money earned helps pay the homeless who work at the center and covers the cost of running it. In addition, We Can works with other groups that provide food, shelter, counseling, and medical care for the homeless.

22

Recycling in School

Does your school recycle garbage? The next time you eat in the school cafeteria, check out what you and your friends are throwing away. Are cans, bottles, and plastic trays going to waste?

Ask your teacher about starting a recycling project at your school. Be sure to mention how much you can learn about the environment by recycling. Your teacher might let your class recycle as a class project.

The first step in a school recycling project is to look in the garbage. Check the garbage cans in your classroom and in the cafeteria. What do you find: paper, cans, bottles? Decide on which items from the garbage you want to recycle.

Step two is to find a place for the garbage. The city government can help you with that. Look in the government section of the phone book or ask a librarian for the address of whoever is in charge of recycling for your community. Sometimes the person is called the "recycling coordinator" or the "environmental coordinator."

Children earn money for projects by collecting beverage cans and bringing them to a recycling center.

The recycling coordinator knows who does recycling in your area. Tell the person what you want to recycle, and he or she will help you find someone to take it—either the city sanitation department or a private company.

Step three is the hard part. You will have to convince the principal and the custodians to let you recycle in school. Tell them what you want to collect. Give them the name of the company or city department that will take the items you collect. You must plan what to do with your materials. No custodian wants the school filling up with paper and empty cans!

Show the principal a plan explaining who will do the work of recycling. Get lots of kids to volunteer to help. Ask teachers to let you tell kids in other classes about your program.

Now comes the fun part. Start recycling! Get recycling containers—trash cans, bins, or buckets—and put one by every trash can. Put signs on the recycling containers to tell people what to put in each one. And put signs on the trash cans: *Trash Only. Do Not Put Recyclable Paper or Cans in Here!*

Recycling will succeed if you make it just as easy to recycle as it is to put stuff in the trash. Make sure you have plenty of recycling containers. Keep recyclable materials in the containers, not littered around them.

A school recycling program is like a small version of a city recycling program. By recycling at your school, you can learn about the problems and rewards that a city faces when it tries to recycle.

Reducing Waste

While recycling can help cut down on trash, it can never get rid of it entirely. Some products are difficult or impossible to recycle. For example, a cardboard milk carton is made of a layer of cardboard tightly attached to a layer of plastic. Separating the two layers is very hard. Juice boxes have many layers of plastic, paper, and aluminum foil. They aren't easily recyclable, either.

"Source reduction" is the name for trying to cut down on waste by reducing the amount of material used in the first place. Aluminum companies have been reducing the amount of metal in aluminum cans for years. The amount of tin on steel cans has also gone down since cans were invented. The layer of tin on a modern can is thinner than a human hair!

But you don't have to own a can factory to do source reduction. The next time you go to the store, look at each package of food you buy and compare packages. You could buy a frozen dinner in a cardboard box. But inside the box is a metal tray with a plastic wrapper. That's a lot of garbage for one meal. If you buy the same item in a can, you only have to throw away one thing, and you get enough food for several people. Of course, if you buy fresh, loose fruits and vegetables, you reduce packaging even more, especially if you bring your own storage bags.

Maybe a package of juice boxes is in your shopping cart. That's several non-recyclable drink containers, some little plastic straws with wrappers, and a layer of plastic covering the whole package. And each box holds only a few ounces of juice. Better to get a can of frozen juice, mix it in a pitcher, and then fill a thermos to take to school.

Getting Creative

The Chicago artist Greg Warmack calls himself "Mr. Imagination" because of the works he creates from garbage. Warmack has built himself a throne from scrap wood covered with bottle caps. Other works include little people made from old, clogged paintbrushes.

Carhenge: A visit to Stonehenge, England, inspired engineer Jim Reinders to build a replica of the famous monument on his farm in Alliance, Nebraska.

25

You can be a creative recycler too. It's easy. You may already have made a simple telephone. All you need is two steel cans and a long piece of string. Punch a small hole in the bottom of each can and run the string through. Tie knots at each end to keep it from slipping back. Have a friend hold one can, then pull the other and stretch the string tight. Hold your ear to the can—keeping the string tight—and listen. You should be able to hear everything your friend says into the other can.

The telephone is easy to make. The projects in this book are a little harder. Later, when you have learned new ways to use metal trash, try to think of your own projects. Wilbur and Orville Wright used an empty tomato can to make part of the engine for the first airplane. Maybe you will invent something, too.

2 CRAFT IT!

Each day, objects containing different forms and shapes of metal are discarded from every home. Metal can be found in things as small as the buttons on a jacket worn beyond use or as large as wrecked automobiles or appliances headed for the junkyard. Discarded things such as coat hangers, cans, pie plates, pipes, bottle caps, bent nails, nuts and bolts, sewing machines, stoves, and door hinges all contain steel, aluminum, copper, brass, or other metals.

Put a carton in a closet or a spare corner where you can keep a collection of these items. Then you won't have far to look when you're ready to create a metal crafts project. But if you need an item not found at home, ask for discards from relatives and neighbors who are remodeling their homes; or talk to managers of construction sites, hardware and lumber stores, and home improvement centers who may be willing to give you scraps that they would otherwise throw away.

You play a part in the recycling of metal in your home when you separate the various types of metal for collection. You can also reuse metal objects by making new things from the metal contained in old ones. These can be practical household items or decorative objects that please the eye. They may be designed for gift giving or used as toys. The possibilities for reusing metal discards are unlimited.

Some projects are suggested in the chart on p. 30 to give you ideas on where to find useful metals and how to put them to work again. In the projects that follow, detailed instructions describe how to make toys, ornaments, games, jewelry, and musical instruments, as well as practical items.

Before you begin work, think your recycling project all the way through, making sure that you take full advantage of the materials that you know how to handle safely. And by all means, make use of your imagination. Even when you are following the instructions given for these projects, you can be thinking of new ones of your own.

YOUR TOOL KIT

A kit of basic hand tools is all you need to do recycling projects with metal. You will be able to complete any of the projects suggested or described in this book if you have the following tools:

1. A hacksaw for cutting pipes, strips, or other solid metal forms.

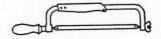

2. A vise for holding metal while you cut it with a hacksaw or file it.

3. Heavy-duty side-cutting pliers for cutting and bending wire.

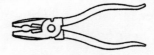

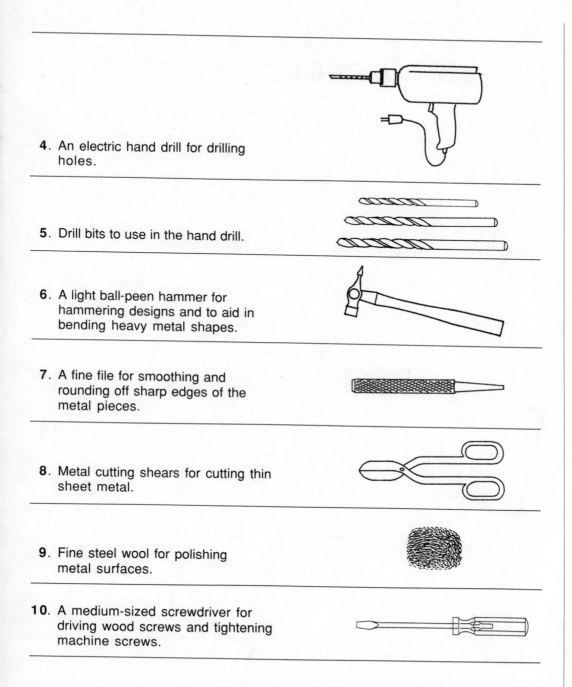

4. An electric hand drill for drilling holes.

5. Drill bits to use in the hand drill.

6. A light ball-peen hammer for hammering designs and to aid in bending heavy metal shapes.

7. A fine file for smoothing and rounding off sharp edges of the metal pieces.

8. Metal cutting shears for cutting thin sheet metal.

9. Fine steel wool for polishing metal surfaces.

10. A medium-sized screwdriver for driving wood screws and tightening machine screws.

Observe all safety rules as you join in the very important effort of reducing waste and making good use of the earth's resources.

METAL RECYCLING IDEAS

Here are some general ideas for discarded metals that you can find around your home and how you can recycle them in projects that are fun and useful. In many cases, the metals can be used in assemblages, art works made from junk, scraps, and odds and ends.

METAL TYPES	SOURCES & NOTES	SUGGESTED REUSES
Aluminum foil	Food wrap or containers; wash thoroughly	Decorative magnets, hanging ornaments, toy coverings, and container linings
Ball bearings	Wheel bearings and machines	Balancing weights, game pieces, and toys
Bolts and nuts	Toys, machinery, and appliances	Use to put projects together; game pieces, weights, and hammer
Bottle, jar, or can tops	Food and other packages; wash	Containers, dollhouse furniture, wheels for toys and tops
Buttons	Uniforms and other clothing	Ornaments, accessories for dollhouses, and toy parts
Coat hangers	Closets, cleaners, and laundromats	Hooks, mobile frames, axles, hangers, and parts of toys
Cookie cutters	Aluminum	Pull toys
Cookie sheets	Steel or aluminum; wash	Drip catchers, paint trays, and bench top protectors
Cooking pots	Steel or aluminum; wash	Planters, bulk storage, and paint-mixing containers
Disposable pie plates	Aluminum; wash thoroughly	Decorative magnets, ornaments, seed planters
Flatware	Forks and spoons	Jewelry items, key fobs, pendants, rings, fishing lures, handles, and wind chimes
Ice-cube trays	Aluminum	Toy boats or storage containers
Lamp base	Brass	Ornamental candleholder

METAL TYPES	SOURCES & NOTES	SUGGESTED REUSES
Large cans	Coffee or paint thinner; wash	Mailbox, colonial lantern, birdhouses, or storage containers
Nails	Furniture, buildings; straighten	Use to put projects together; tools for leather-work and axles for toys.
Paper clips	Steel wire or flat brass	Make chains, hangers, jewelry, and dollhouse accessories
Pie tins	Steel; wash thoroughly	Pinwheels, storage containers, seed planter trays, and noisemakers
Pipes and fittings	Plumbing	Furniture frames, toys, and candleholders
Pot lids	Aluminum	Work trays and noisemakers
Radio antenna	Automobile whip type	Fishing pole
Safety pins	Steel	Use in mobiles, jewelry, hooks, fishing lures, and hangers
Screws	Furniture	Use to put projects together; game pieces
Small cans	Food packaging; wash to clean	Storage containers, tin can telephones, rhythm music makers, and noisemakers
Strip metal	Door grills	Weather vanes, coat racks, and toys
Structural forms	Channels, angles, I beams	Furniture, mountings, and playground equipment
Thick sheet metal	Radio cabinets, instrument panels	Windmill blades or whirligigs
Thin sheet metal	Roof flashing, shim stock, brass, copper, aluminum	Ornaments, earrings, decorative magnets, mobiles, and hammered jewelry.
Tubing	Electric conduit, copper plumbing	Wind chimes, whistles, and toy parts
Umbrella ribs	Steel or aluminum	Mobile frames, hangers, or bent handles
Wire	Coat hangers and electric cable	Make chains, axles, jewelry links, and mobile frames

"NUTTY" CHESS/CHECKERS GAME SET

Nuts, bolts, and screws are abundant and cheap. They are used to hold almost everything together, but they are often wasted and discarded needlessly. When the things they hold together are worn out and thrown away, the nuts, bolts, and screws are seldom removed, even though they are still in good condition and could be used again. An assortment of modified nuts, bolts, and screws can be recycled to be used as the pieces for playing checkers and chess. A recycled cookie tin serves both as the playing surface for the chess and checker games and as a storage container for the pieces between games—great for taking along on a trip!

MATERIALS

- 24 wood screws 1/2" long (checkers and pawns)
- 14 size 1/4"-20 hexagonal nuts (rooks, queens' crowns, knights' bodies, and bishops' bases)
- 2 size 1/4"-20 wing nuts (kings' crowns)
- 4 size 1/4"-20 flat-head machine screws 3/4" long (knights)
- 4 size 1/4"-20 flat-head machine screws 1" long (kings and queens)
- 4 size 1/4"-20 round-head machine screws 3/4" long (bishops)
- 4 small nails 3/4" long (knights' lances)
- Nontoxic adhesive, such as Elmer's SAF-T Contact Cement
- Black and white paint

TOOLS

- Black felt-tip pen
- Paintbrush
- Ruler

INSTRUCTIONS

1. The 1/2" wood screws are used as they are for the 24 checkers and/or the 16 pawns of the chess set. Four of the hexagonal nuts are rooks. Make the other chess pieces by gluing the nuts and machine screws together:

    for the two kings, glue 1"-long flat-head machine screws to wing nuts;

    for the two queens, glue 1"-long flat-head machine screws to hexagonal nuts;

    for the four knights, glue 3/4"-long machine screws to hexagonal nuts and glue nail "lance" to each nut;

    for the four bishops, glue round-head machine screws to hexagonal nuts.

2. Paint half the pieces black. Then paint the rest white.

3. Paint lid of cookie tin white.

4. Draw a 5" square on lid with the felt-tip pen.

5. Draw lines with ruler across the square 5/8" apart in both directions to form 64 small squares. Color half the squares black, and leave the others white in a typical checker-board pattern.

VARIATIONS

Search your toolbox for your own combinations of bolts, screws, and nuts to make interesting chess pieces.

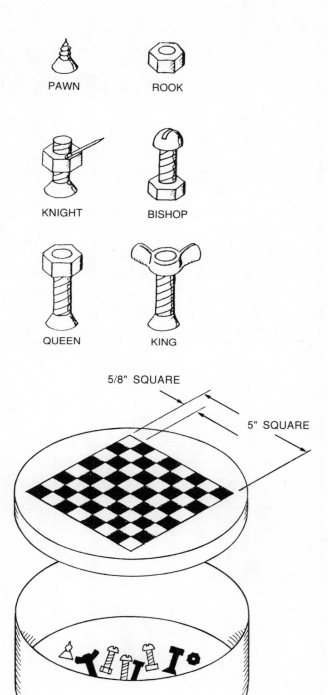

PAWN   ROOK

KNIGHT   BISHOP

QUEEN   KING

5/8" SQUARE

5" SQUARE

BATTLING FINGER TOPS

Finger tops are the small tops that you spin between your thumb and forefinger to make them go. Almost every toy or household machine that is broken or worn out has metal wheels or contains gears that can be recycled to make finger tops. Even bottle lids or plain metal disks can be recycled. All you have to do is mount a nail through the exact center of the wheel, gear, or other metal disk. When you flip the top with fingers and put it down on the floor or a table, it will spin on the pointed end of the nail. Other recycled nails standing on their heads on a table or in a box become the targets as tops score by knocking them down or by knocking one another off balance.

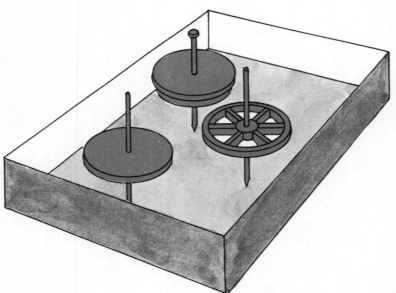

MATERIALS

- Various metal disks in the form of wheels from toys, gears, or bottle lids
- Nails of assorted diameters and lengths
- Nontoxic adhesive, such as Elmer's SAF-T Contact Cement
- Variety of paints

TOOLS

- Hacksaw
- Vise
- Hammer
- Pointed nail
- Fine file
- Paintbrush

SAFETY NOTE: When sawing any metal, take every precaution not to injure yourself on the blade and the rough edges of the sawed-off metal.

INSTRUCTIONS

1. Select a nail to fit the central hole of a wheel or gear.

2. Saw off head from nail

3. File cut end of nail smooth.

4. Glue the disk to the nail near pointed end.

5. Use pointed nail and hammer to punch a hole in center of bottle lids, or to enlarge the hole in other wheels or disks that are too small for the nails.

6. Paint geometric shapes or designs on the tops.

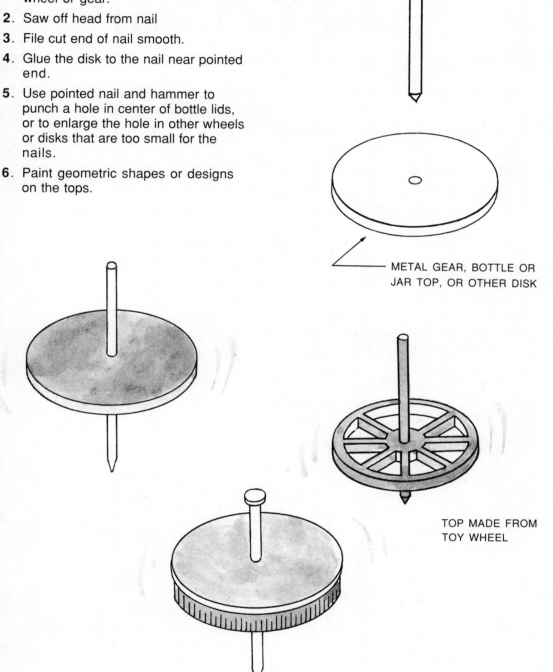

← NAIL WITH HEAD CUT OFF

METAL GEAR, BOTTLE OR JAR TOP, OR OTHER DISK

TOP MADE FROM TOY WHEEL

35

DOLLHOUSE
TABLE AND CHAIRS

By using the lids of empty jars or bottles for the top of the table and the seats of the chairs, you can make a mini toy table and chair set. Nails are used for the legs of the table and the chairs. The backrests of the chairs are bent from wire. The table and chairs are similar to old-fashioned ice-cream-parlor furniture, and are suitable for use on the patio of a 1"-scale dollhouse. They can be painted any color, but the chairs and table look especially smart when painted white.

MATERIALS

- One jar lid, 3 1/2" in diameter, for tabletop
- One bottle top, 2" in diameter, for each chair's seat
- Four nails 3" long, for table legs
- Four nails 2" long, for each chair's legs
- One wire coat hanger
- Nontoxic adhesive, such as Elmer's SAF-T Contact Cement
- White paint

TOOLS

- Heavy-duty side-cutting pliers
- Hacksaw
- Vise
- Fine file
- Hammer
- Pointed nail
- Paintbrush
- Large sharp nail

SAFETY NOTE: When sawing any metal, take every precaution not to injure yourself on the blade and the rough edges of the sawed-off metal.

INSTRUCTIONS

1. Make a crossmark inside each lid to locate the position of the legs.

2. Saw off four nails 2 1/2" long to make the legs of the table. Cut four nails 1 1/2" long to make the legs for each chair. (Place nails horizontally with pointed ends in vise, and use hacksaw to cut.)

3. File cut ends of nails smooth.

4. Glue heads of nails under the lids, using the crossmarks as a guide for position.

5. Use the hammer and sharp nail to punch two holes in the seat of the chair for the backrest.

6. Using pliers, cut a piece of coat-hanger wire 6" long.

7. Curve the wire to make a half loop with straight sides. Bend ends of wire at a sharp angle.

8. Push ends of wire through the punched holes in chair seat.

9. Glue bent ends in place under seat.

10. Paint table and chairs.

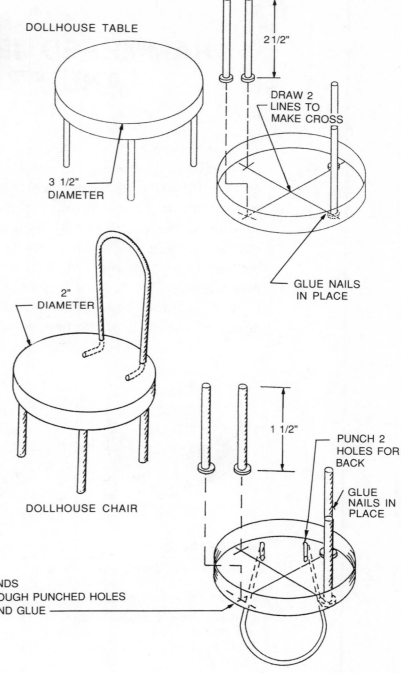

DOLLHOUSE TABLE

3 1/2" DIAMETER

2 1/2"

DRAW 2 LINES TO MAKE CROSS

GLUE NAILS IN PLACE

2" DIAMETER

DOLLHOUSE CHAIR

1 1/2"

PUNCH 2 HOLES FOR BACK

GLUE NAILS IN PLACE

SHARP BENDS
PUSH THROUGH PUNCHED HOLES IN SEAT, AND GLUE

HAMMERED JEWELRY TRAY
AND BRACELET

Thin sheet metal is sometimes available from old instrument cabinets, radio equipment, or similar sources. Some sheet metals are quite soft, while others are very hard. The softer metals, such as aluminum and copper, are relatively easy to deform or shape by hammering on their surface. By hammering tiny dents on flat sheets of soft metal, you can produce an interesting and varied design pattern on the surface. Hammered objects like this jewelry tray and bracelet make distinctive recycling projects, because their individual patterns and final shape are controlled by the way the hammering is done and the skill of the person who makes them.

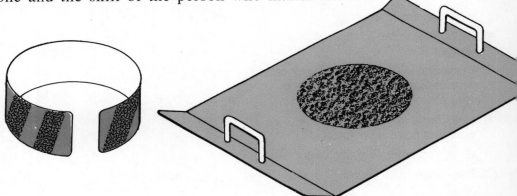

MATERIALS

- Aluminum or copper sheet metal 1/32" to 1/16" (You may use cookie sheet if at least 1/32" thick.)
- Aluminum wire approximately 1/8" in diameter

TOOLS

- Metal-cutting shears
- Fine file
- Small, lightweight ball peen hammer
- Flat block of steel
- Fine steel wool
- Electric hand drill
- 1/8"-diameter drill bit
- Heavy-duty side-cutting pliers

SAFETY NOTE: Use power tools only with adult supervision.

INSTRUCTIONS

1. Using shears, cut a strip of sheet metal 1" long and 7" wide to make bracelet. Cut another piece of sheet metal 4" wide and 6" long to make jewelry tray.

2. File edges and corners of metal pieces to remove all sharp surfaces and make them smooth.

3. Draw a design pattern on each piece of metal.

4. Hold the piece of metal flat on the heavy steel block, with pattern side turned up.

5. Use the round (ball peen) end of the hammerhead to tap the metal gently to make the pattern. Do not strike the metal with heavy blows. Start near the center of the pattern and work your way out toward the edges.

6. Polish metal pieces with fine steel wool.

7. Using pliers, bend bracelet to shape.

8. Bend the ends of the tray up slightly.

9. Drill four holes in tray for handles.

10. Using pliers, cut two pieces of wire 2" long.

11. Bend wire to make handles.

12. Put handles through holes in the tray. Bend ends back to hold in place.

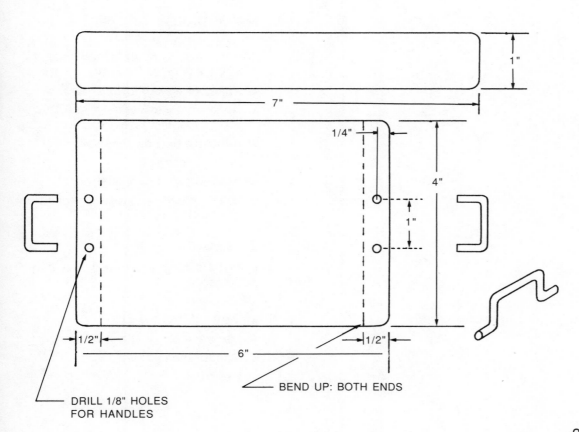

DRILL 1/8" HOLES
FOR HANDLES

BEND UP: BOTH ENDS

39

HANGING ORNAMENTS AND DECORATIVE MAGNETS

Thin pieces of sheet metal made of aluminum, copper, or brass are often thought to have no value because they are so small. In fact, the metal from throwaway aluminum pie plates, baking pans, copper roof flashing, and similar sources can be recycled to make decorations that are pretty and colorful. Bright ornaments made by recycling thin metal are useful as hanging Christmas decorations, or they may be mounted on adhesive-backed magnetic strip. This way, they are useful for decorating refrigerators, school lockers, metal cabinets, and bulletin boards.

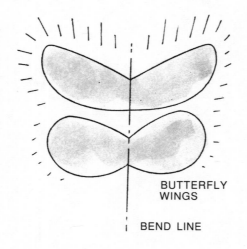

BUTTERFLY WINGS

BEND LINE

MATERIALS

- Very thin sheet metal, such as aluminum throwaway pie plates, copper roof flashing, or brass shim stock
- Paints of various colors
- Nontoxic adhesive, such as Elmer's SAF-T Contact Cement
- Adhesive-backed magnetic strip
- Wire paper clips
- Tracing paper (optional)
- Graphite carbon paper, or equivalent (optional)

TOOLS

- Metal-cutting shears or heavy-duty scissors
- Very fine file
- Very fine steel wool
- Large needle or sharp nail
- Paintbrushes
- Pencil

MAGNET STRIP

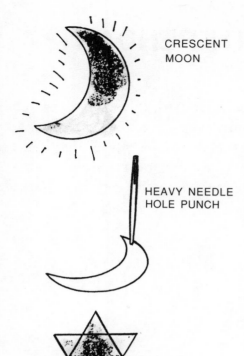

CRESCENT
MOON

HEAVY NEEDLE
HOLE PUNCH

SIX-POINT STAR

PANSY

FIVE-POINT STAR

INSTRUCTIONS

1. Draw your own designs. Or, if you wish, trace drawings from the book by placing tracing paper over them and trace with pencil. Place graphite (or carbon) transfer paper, graphite side down, on the thin sheet metal. Then trace pattern with pencil. (If you don't have any graphite paper, you can make your own by using the side of a pencil tip to stroke heavily and evenly back and forth covering one side of a piece of white paper.)

2. Cut the parts out.

3. File edges to smooth them.

4. Polish with very fine steel wool.

5. If the ornament has more than one part, glue parts together.

6. For hanging ornaments, make a hole with the heavy needle or sharp nail; then paint (if desired), and hang from a paper clip.

7. For magnets, cut a 1/2" piece of adhesive-backed magnetic strip, peel off backing paper, and stick the magnet to the ornament.

VARIATIONS

Glue on sequins, sparkles, or other trim for colorful ornaments.

KEY RING WITH PENDANT

Stainless-steel or silver-plated spoons and forks become scratched and dull during their normal lifetime. They are also often bent by being jammed in drawers or dishwashers. After a while, they tend to get discarded. When that happens, they can be recycled to make unusual key-ring pendants. Initialed pendants are especially attractive as gifts.

MATERIALS

- One key ring
- One fork or spoon
- Very fine steel wool

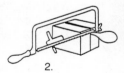

2.

TOOLS

- Hacksaw
- Vise
- Fine file
- Electric hand drill
- 3/16"-diameter drill bit

3.

4.

SAFETY NOTE: Use power tools only with adult supervision. When sawing any metal, take every precaution not to injure yourself on the blade and the rough edges of the sawed-off metal.

INSTRUCTIONS

1. Polish handle of spoon or fork with steel wool.
2. Saw off a 2" piece from end of handle.
3. File cut end of piece to round it off.
4. Drill a hole through piece 1/4" from cut end.
5. Slip the key ring through the hole in the piece.

WHISTLE

Copper is one of the most beautiful metals because of its rich color. It is very useful for making pipes and anything else that is exposed to water, because it does not rust, and it lasts for a long time. Copper is a soft metal that is easy to cut and bend. The size referred to in dealing with copper pipes is the inside diameter.

A short piece of 1/2" copper pipe can be recycled into a loud whistle. The mouthpiece of the whistle is made by shaping a cork and putting it in one end of the whistle. The opposite end of the whistle is sealed by another cork. The length of the whistle determines its pitch—how high or low its note is.

MATERIALS

- One piece of 1/2" copper pipe
- Two 1/2"-diameter corks
- Nontoxic adhesive, such as Elmer's SAF-T Contact Cement

TOOLS

- Hacksaw
- Vise
- Thin fine file
- Fine steel wool

SAFETY NOTE: When sawing any metal, take every precaution not to injure yourself on the blade and the rough edges of the sawed-off metal.

INSTRUCTIONS

1. Saw off a piece of pipe 4 1/2" long.
2. File both ends of pipe to make them smooth.

3. Polish pipe with steel wool.

4. File an opening 1/8" deep x 5/16" wide in side of pipe 1 1/8" from end for the mouthpiece.

5. Wash pipe thoroughly with soap and water to be sure it is clean, dry, and free of all metal chips.

6. File a flat side on one of the corks.

7. Glue flat-sided cork in place in the mouthpiece of the whistle.

8. Glue other cork in opposite end of whistle.

Now have yourself a toot!

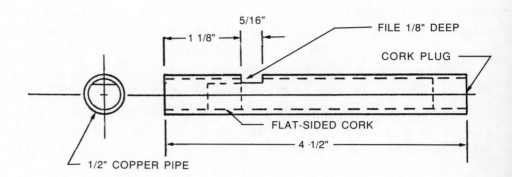

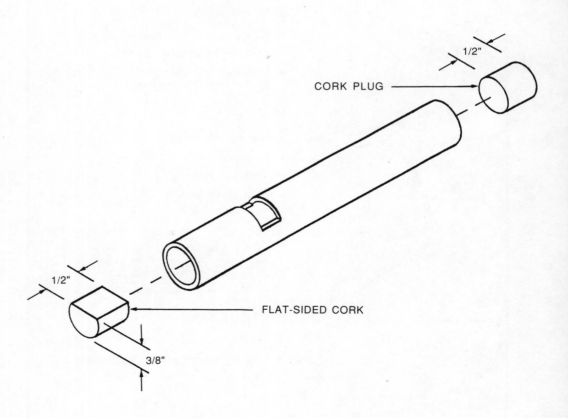

BONGO DRUMS

Musical instruments do not have to be complicated to make. Simple things like empty food cans can be recycled into bongo drums. They are interesting instruments that anyone can play with their finger-tips. Although not capable of producing elaborate musical sounds, bongo drums can be used to create varied drumbeat rhythms. By re-cycling two coffee cans of different sizes, you can make a set of drums that will give different pitches or tones, depending upon the sizes of the cans and the end used as the head.

MATERIALS

- Two coffee cans of different sizes with snap-on lids
- Colored vinyl tape
- Paint

TOOLS

- Scissors
- Paintbrush

INSTRUCTIONS

1. Snap plastic lid on open end of can to close it.
2. Cut a piece of vinyl tape long enough to go all the way around can.
3. Run tape around edge of can to secure lid.
4. Cut two pieces of vinyl tape long enough to go around both cans.
5. Tape cans together at top and bottom.
6. Paint drums with a colorful design.

TWO SIZES OF COFFEE CANS

VINYL TAPE SECURES TOP TO CANS

VINYL TAPE BINDS CANS TOGETHER

TIN CAN MARACAS

Maracas are rhythm instruments that are played in pairs and impart a special sound to Latin American music. Two empty food cans can be recycled to make a pair of maracas by attaching a handle to each one and sealing some dried beans inside. The player holds one of the maracas in each hand and shakes them like rattles in rhythm with the music. When played with Latin-style music, tin can maracas make a pleasant sound that adds to the background effect.

MATERIALS
- Two food cans of about 1-lb capacity
- Dried beans
- Two wooden dowels 1/2" in diameter and 6" long
- Two round-head wood screws 3/4" long
- Colored vinyl tape
- Thin cardboard
- Paint

TOOLS
- Hammer
- Pointed nail
- Screwdriver
- Paintbrush

INSTRUCTIONS

1. Punch hole in center of bottom of each can with the hammer and pointed nail.

2. Drive a screw through hole into end of one of the dowels for a handle.

3. Cut two cardboard circles to fit open ends of the cans.

4. Place 12 dried beans in each can.

5. Place a cardboard circle over open end of each can.

6. Tape cardboard circle in place by running tape around edge of can.

7. Paint the maracas.

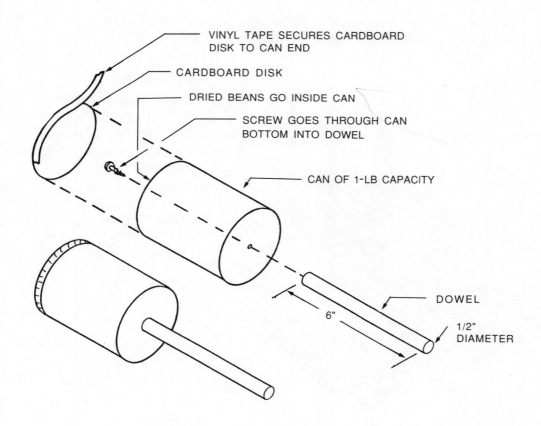

VINYL TAPE SECURES CARDBOARD DISK TO CAN END

CARDBOARD DISK

DRIED BEANS GO INSIDE CAN

SCREW GOES THROUGH CAN BOTTOM INTO DOWEL

CAN OF 1-LB CAPACITY

DOWEL

6"

1/2" DIAMETER

47

DESK ORGANIZER

This is a very practical project. Short metal pieces cut from pipes, electrical conduit, or other forms of steel or aluminum tubing can make the compartments of a neat desk organizer for storing pens, pencils, rulers, and so on. Lids taken from empty jars hold paper clips, rubber bands, postage stamps, and other small things that are lost easily. Letters are stacked neatly on edge between frames that are bent from the wire available in old coat hangers. All of the parts are mounted on a wooden base to make a bright, attractive desk unit.

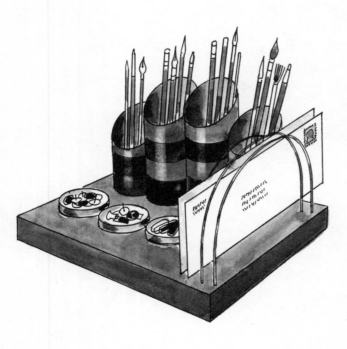

MATERIALS

- One piece of metal tubing about 1 1/2" in diameter
- Three wire coat hangers
- Three metal jar lids about 2" in diameter
- One piece of wood 6" wide, 8" long, and 3/4" thick
- Nontoxic adhesive, such as Elmer's SAF-T Contact Cement
- Colored vinyl tape

TOOLS

- Hacksaw
- Vise
- Heavy-duty side-cutting pliers
- Electric hand drill
- 3/32"-diameter drill bit
- Fine file
- Paintbrush

SAFETY NOTE: Use power tools only with adult supervision. When sawing any metal, take every precaution not to injure yourself on the blade and the rough edges of the sawed-off metal.

INSTRUCTIONS

1. Using pliers, cut three pieces of wire 12" long from the straight parts of the coat hangers.

2. File ends of wires to make them smooth.

3. Using pliers, bend the pieces of wire so they have straight sides and are curved across the top.

4. Saw off two pieces of pipe 3" long and two pieces 4" long. Cut them straight across the bottom end and at an angle across top end.

5. File ends of pipe pieces to make them smooth.

6. Wrap strips of colored vinyl tape around pipes to decorate them brightly.

7. Drill six holes in the wooden base for the letter rack.

8. Push one end of a curved wire into one of the drilled holes in the base. Push opposite end of wire into opposite hole.

9. Repeat step 8 with other two wires.

10. Glue pieces of pipe and jar lids in place on base.

11. Paint the parts that have not been covered with vinyl tape.

VARIATIONS

Use various-sized tin cans instead of pipes. Paint them, then nail them in place on the board.

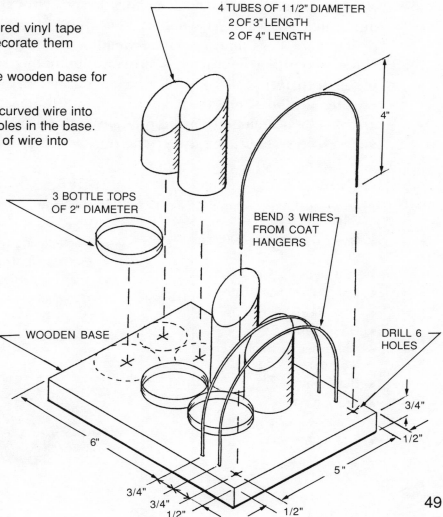

4 TUBES OF 1 1/2" DIAMETER
2 OF 3" LENGTH
2 OF 4" LENGTH

4"

3 BOTTLE TOPS
OF 2" DIAMETER

BEND 3 WIRES
FROM COAT
HANGERS

WOODEN BASE

DRILL 6
HOLES

3/4"

1/2"

6"

5"

3/4"

3/4"

1/2"

1/2"

49

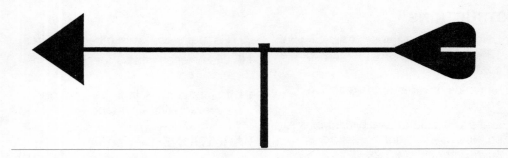

ARROW WEATHER VANE

Aluminum is a metal that does not rust, which makes it excellent for outdoor items such as weather vanes and storm doors, because it resists dampness and other bad-weather conditions. Another way to make something new from a broken aluminum storm door is using the grill to form the body of a weather vane. Arrowhead and feather profiles are cut from sheet aluminum and bolted to the body of the arrow. When mounted on the pipe up high out of doors, the weather vane always shows the direction from which the wind is blowing.

MATERIALS

- One piece of aluminum grill strip 1/2" wide
- One piece of sheet aluminum 1/16" thick
- Two small bolts and nuts
- One 1/4"-20 bolt 6" long
- Two 1/4"-20 nuts
- One washer
- One piece of small-diameter (1/8" - 3/8") pipe 2' long
- Black paint
- Tracing paper
- Graphite carbon paper
- Cardboard

TOOLS

- Hacksaw
- Vise
- Metal-cutting shears
- Electric hand drill
- 3/16"-diameter drill bit
- 1/4"-diameter drill bit
- Screwdriver
- Paintbrush
- Pencil

SAFETY NOTE: Use power tools only with adult supervision. When sawing any metal, take every precaution not to injure yourself on the blade and the rough edges of the sawed-off metal.

INSTRUCTIONS

1. Saw off a piece of aluminum grill strip 20" long.

2. File ends of strip to make them smooth.

3. Drill a 3/16" hole 1" from each end and a 1/4" hole at center of strip.

4. Using tracing paper, copy patterns for arrowhead and feathers. With graphite (or carbon paper), trace patterns to cardboard. (If you don't have any graphite paper, you can make your own by using the side of a pencil tip to stroke heavily and evenly back and forth covering one side of a piece of white paper.) Then transfer pattern to the metal.

5. Using shears, cut two half arrowheads and two feathers from aluminum sheet.

6. File edges of sheet-metal pieces to make them smooth.

7. Drill a 3/16" hole near edge of each sheet metal piece.

8. Bend a 1/2" flange on each sheet metal piece.

9. Using small bolts, bolt the sheet metal pieces to the strip to make the arrow. Tighten bolts with screwdriver.

10. Saw off head from 1/4" bolt.

11. File end of bolt to make it smooth.

12. Put bolt in center hole of the arrow with a nut on each side of arrow.

13. Paint the arrow.

14. Put the bolt in arrow through the washer over end of pipe.

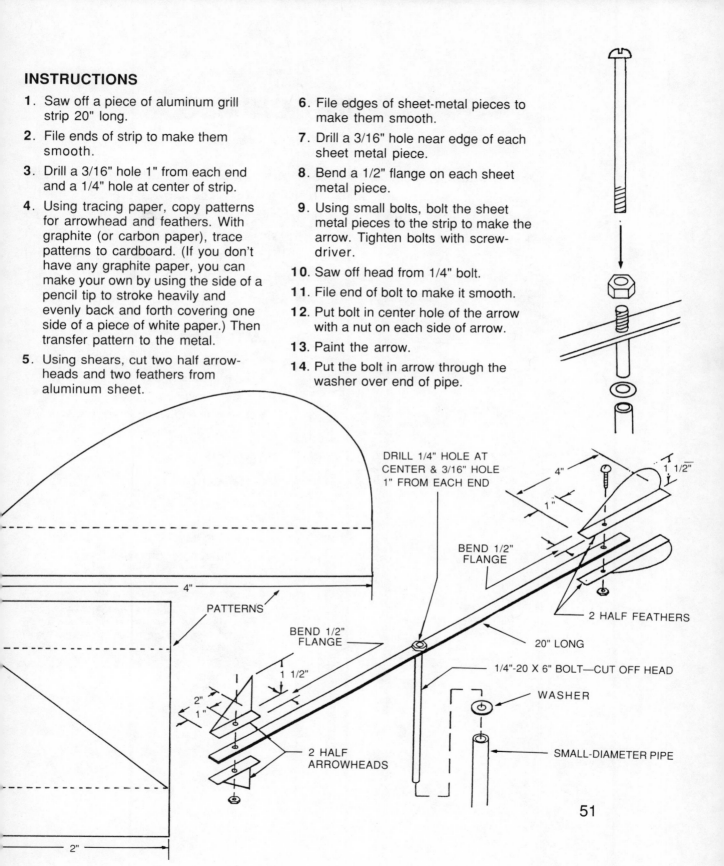

DRILL 1/4" HOLE AT CENTER & 3/16" HOLE 1" FROM EACH END

4"

1"

1 1/2"

BEND 1/2" FLANGE

2 HALF FEATHERS

20" LONG

1/4"-20 X 6" BOLT—CUT OFF HEAD

WASHER

SMALL-DIAMETER PIPE

2 HALF ARROWHEADS

BEND 1/2" FLANGE

1 1/2"

2"

1"

PATTERNS

4"

2"

51

WIND CHIMES

Some metals, such as steel, are quite hard and tough; other metals, such as aluminum and lead, are quite soft. The harder pieces of metal make a ringing sound like a bell when they are struck. You can make a set of wind chimes by recycling short pieces of steel tubing. If you set this up where the wind can blow it and make it swing back and forth, the pieces of recycled tubing will bump against one another and give a pleasant chiming sound.

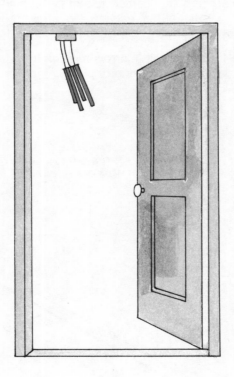

MATERIALS

- A length of 1"-diameter steel tubing
- Five pieces of string
- One screw eye
- One piece of wood 2" square and 3/4" thick

TOOLS

- Hacksaw
- Vise
- Fine file
- Electric hand drill
- 1/8"-diameter drill bit

SAFETY NOTE: Use power tools only with adult supervision. When sawing any metal, take every precaution not to injure yourself on the blade and the rough edges of the sawed-off metal.

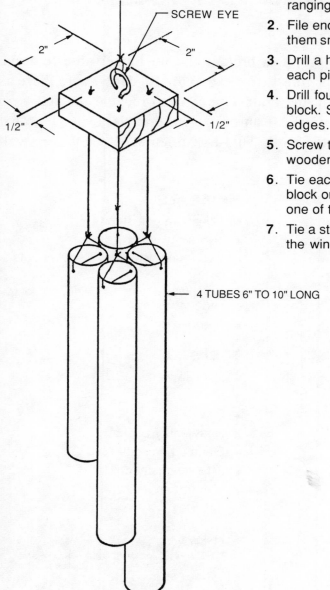

SCREW EYE

2"

2"

1/2"

1/2"

4 TUBES 6" TO 10" LONG

INSTRUCTIONS

1. Saw off four pieces of steel tubing ranging from 6" to 10" long.

2. File ends of four pieces to make them smooth.

3. Drill a hole through both sides of each piece of tubing 1/4" from end.

4. Drill four holes through the wooden block. Space the holes 1/2" from edges.

5. Screw the screw eye into center of wooden block.

6. Tie each piece of tubing to wooden block on a 6" piece of string through one of the holes.

7. Tie a string to the screw eye to hang the wind chimes.

COAT AND HAT RACK

When an aluminum storm door is broken and no longer able to serve its original purpose, it is likely to be discarded. However, there is always strong metal left in the door. One way to recycle the flat strip metal from the protective grill of an old storm door is to make a coat and hat rack to hang on the wall. This is a practical item that is well worth making.

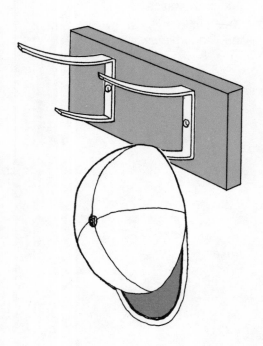

MATERIALS

- Aluminum grill strip
- Two screw eyes
- Two round-head wood screws 3/4" long
- One piece of wood 4" wide, 10" long, and 3/4" thick
- Paint

TOOLS

- Hacksaw
- Vise
- Fine file
- Heavy-duty pliers
- Electric hand drill
- 3/16"-diameter drill bit
- Paintbrush

SAFETY NOTE: Use power tools only with adult supervision. When sawing any metal, take every precaution not to injure yourself on the blade and the rough edges of the sawed-off metal.

INSTRUCTIONS

1. Saw off two pieces of aluminum strip 10" long.

2. File ends of strips to round them off.

3. Drill a hole through each strip 3 1/2" from end.

4. Bend an angle 2" from end of each strip near hole, and another angle 5" from opposite end.

5. Drive the screw eyes into the edge of the wood 2" from ends.

6. Drive a wood screw through the hole in each strip, to attach strips to front of wood 2" from ends.

7. Curve ends of strip up slightly.

8. Paint the coat and hat rack, and hang it on the wall by passing two sturdy screws or nails through the screw eyes.

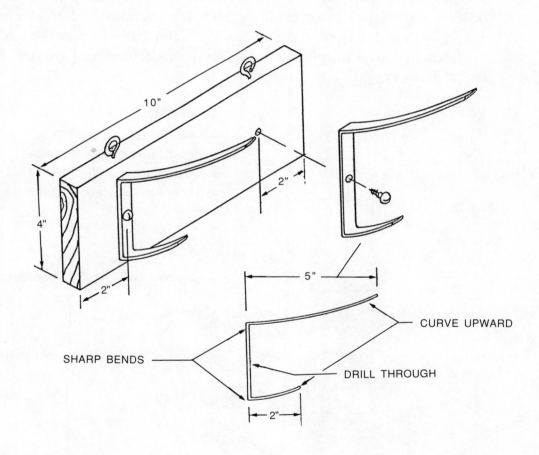

10"

4"

2"

2"

5"

2"

CURVE UPWARD

SHARP BENDS

DRILL THROUGH

CANDLEHOLDER

Pipe fittings and other materials from plumbing work are often applied for various uses not related to water supply or heating systems. This is because iron pipes and pipe fittings are strong, simple to use, and available in many standard sizes. Pipes that are called "half-inch size" are actually larger than that. If you measure a 1/2" iron or steel pipe, you will find that its outside diameter is nearly 7/8". Of course, the elbows and other fittings that go with it are larger still in order for the pipes to screw into them. By obtaining a few pieces of 1/2" pipe materials that are no longer needed, it is possible to recycle them into a decorative and useful candleholder. This size pipe fits the average-sized candle.

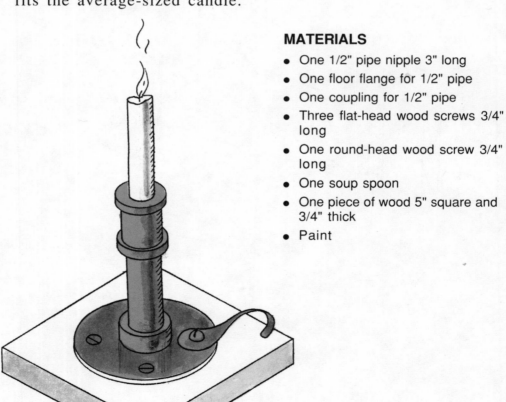

MATERIALS

- One 1/2" pipe nipple 3" long
- One floor flange for 1/2" pipe
- One coupling for 1/2" pipe
- Three flat-head wood screws 3/4" long
- One round-head wood screw 3/4" long
- One soup spoon
- One piece of wood 5" square and 3/4" thick
- Paint

56

TOOLS

- Screwdriver
- Hacksaw
- Vise
- Fine file
- Electric hand drill
- 3/16"-diameter drill bit
- Heavy-duty pliers
- Hammer
- Pointed nail
- Paintbrush

INSTRUCTIONS

1. Saw off handle from spoon close to the bowl of the spoon.
2. File cut end of spoon handle smooth.
3. Drill a hole near the center of wide part of spoon handle.
4. Using pliers, bend spoon handle to make a carrying handle for the candleholder.
5. Position floor flange in center of wooden base.
6. Mark locations of the screw holes on base with a pencil.
7. Punch screw locations with hammer and pointed nail on the base to assist in starting the screws.
8. Drive the flat-head wood screws through three holes in floor flange to attach it to base.
9. Drive round-head wood screw through hole in spoon handle and other hole in floor flange.
10. Screw pipe nipple into floor flange.
11. Screw coupling to top of pipe nipple.
12. Paint the candleholder.

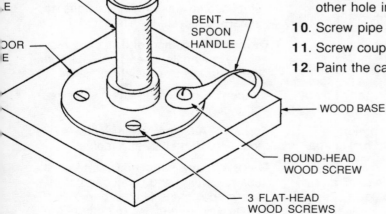

1/2" PIPE COUPLING

3" PIPE ... E

OOR E

BENT SPOON HANDLE

WOOD BASE

ROUND-HEAD WOOD SCREW

3 FLAT-HEAD WOOD SCREWS

DRILL 3/16" HOLE

GLOSSARY

Alloy. A mixture of two or more metals.

Aluminum. A silver-white metal that is lightweight and does not rust; as an alloy, it is strong and hard. It is the most abundant metal on the earth's crust and is used to make cans, housewares, and parts of airplanes and cars.

Archaeologist. A scientist who studies past human life through the material remains of ancient cultures.

Bellows. A device for driving air into a fire or furnace.

Blast furnace. A furnace for smelting ore, in which hot air is driven in under pressure.

Brass. A yellow alloy of copper and zinc used in plumbing fixtures, musical instruments, small machine parts, and decoration.

Bronze. A brownish alloy of copper and tin, once used for most tools and weapons and now used in machine parts, medals, statues, and bells.

Buy-back, or redemption. A recycling program in which people get money for the materials they collect.

Carbon. A nonmetallic element that is present in all living matter. It is important in steelmaking and is part of many fuels, such as coal, coke, and oil.

Cast. To make objects from metal by pouring melted metal into molds and letting it cool.

Charcoal. A black substance made by partly burning wood or other matter in an oven from which air is excluded. As a fuel, it yields a large amount of heat.

Chromium. A hard blue-white metal often used in making stainless steel.

Coke. A hard gray fuel made from heating soft coal. It burns very hot and is used to smelt iron.

Compound. A distinct substance made up of a union of separate elements.

Copper. A soft, reddish metal used mostly to make coins, roofing, wire, and pipes; one of the best conductors of heat and electricity.

Crucible. A pot that can withstand great heat and in which metals are melted.

Curbside. A recycling program in which people put their materials outside to be picked up.

Deposit. An amount of money that is added to the cost of an item and given back when the container is returned to the store. Deposits on cans and bottles are used to reduce littering and encourage recycling.

Detin. To remove the tin from a piece of steel coated with tin. Detinning is necessary to recycle the steel and the tin.

Drop-off. A method of collecting recyclable materials whereby people bring the materials to special collection sites.

Element. One of the parts that makes up a complex whole.

Foundry. A factory where metal is founded, or melted and molded.

Gold. A heavy, soft metal used to make coins, jewelry, and small parts of electronic equipment. Gold is one of the best recycled metals, and one of the most expensive.

Incinerate. To burn garbage, sometimes using the heat to make steam.

Iron. A hard gray metal that rusts and is attracted by magnets. Most iron today is made into steel. In its various forms, it is used for many products, such as machinery, pipes, screws and nuts, chains, cans, appliances, automobiles, trains, planes, and in the construction of bridges and buildings.

Landfill. A place where garbage is buried in giant holes in the ground and covered with soil.

Lead. A heavy, soft, grayish metal used to make battery plates, fishing sinkers, bullets, pipes, and other items. Lead can be toxic, but it also can be used as a protective shield against X-rays.

Mercury. A heavy, silvery, poisonous metal that is liquid at ordinary temperatures. It is used in batteries, various kinds of lamps, thermometers, barometers, and other scientific instruments.

Metal. Any of various mineral substances that is generally opaque (light won't go through it), fusible (can be melted), ductile (capable of being drawn out, as for wire), and lustrous (has a shine). A few examples are bronze, gold, silver, platinum, copper, iron, lead, tin, uranium, zinc, or an alloy of any of these.

Ore. A rock that contains metal. The metal can be removed by smelting.

Platinum. A silver-white precious metal that does not tarnish. It is used to make jewelry and laboratory apparatus.

Precious metal. Gold, silver, or platinum. These metals are so difficult to mine, and so expensive to buy, that they are almost completely recycled. Jewelers and pawnshops buy precious metal items for recycling and reuse.

Recyclable. Able to be reprocessed and reused in either the same form or as part of a different product.

Recycling. Collecting and reprocessing manufactured materials for reuse. There are five steps in effective recycling: collecting waste materials, separating them by type, processing them into reusable forms, marketing the new products, and buying and using the recycled goods.

Silver. A shiny, precious metal used to make eating utensils, jewelry, and coins. It is also used in photography; in most film-developing machines, a set of electric wires collects the leftover silver for recycling.

Smelt. To separate a metal from ore by high heat.

Steel. A strong, flexible alloy of iron, carbon, and sometimes other elements. Today, most steel is produced by one of three methods: the open hearth furnace, the electric furnace, or the basic oxygen furnace.

Sulfuric acid. A strong corrosive acid. It is one of the most widely used industrial chemicals, is important in processing metals, and is found in motor vehicle batteries.

Tin. A soft, silvery metal used to protect tin cans.

Toxic. Poisonous.

Wrought. Beaten or hammered into shape.

Zinc. A soft, silvery metal used in some kinds of batteries and steel.

FIND OUT MORE

In theory almost everything can be recycled, but in practice a lot depends on you and your community. Listed here are the most common items that can be recovered and recycled before they go into the solid waste stream:

Paper. Newspaper, books, magazines, office papers, commercial print, corrugated packaging, folding cartons, cardboard, bags

Glass. Beer/soda bottles, wine/spirits bottles, food containers

Metal. Ferrous metal (iron and steel), including food and beverage cans, appliances, automobiles, aluminum, including soda cans, lead (car batteries), other non-ferrous (such as copper and brass)

Plastic. Plates and cups, clothing and shoes, soft drink bottles, milk bottles, containers, bags, wraps

Rubber. Tires, clothing and shoes

Textiles and *Leather.* Clothing and shoes

Other Organic Material. Food, yard wastes, wood chips

Motor Oil.

Items not easily recyclable are oily rags, household batteries, paper mixed with food, disposable diapers, and other multi-material products that can't readily be separated into reusable materials.

A material is truly recyclable only if there is a recycling system in place. Successful recycling depends upon having the necessary technology to collect, sort, and process recoverable materials, as well as finding a market for them. Your community may be capable of providing programs for only a few of these items. To find recyclers outside your community, look in the yellow pages of a telephone directory under such headings as Recycling Centers, Waste Reduction, Waste Paper, Scrap Metal, etc. for businesses devoted to salvaging waste. However, it may not be economically wise to spend a lot of time and gasoline to find a far-off recycler. Your best bet is to promote and expand existing programs in your community.

60

We would like to acknowledge the following organizations for their help. They can provide you, too, with information to increase your knowledge and help you in your recycling efforts.

Companies and Organizations

Aluminum Co. of America (ALCOA)
1100 Riverview Tower
900 S. Gay St.
Knoxville, TN 37902

The Aluminum Association
900 19th St. NW, Suite 200
Washington, DC 20006
(202) 862-5163

American Iron and Steel Institute
1133 15th St. NW, Suite 300
Washington, DC 20005
(202) 452-7100
Write for *Steelmaking Flowlines*, a detailed chart of how steel is made and how scrap steel is reborn.

Can Manufacturers Institute
1625 Massachusetts Ave. NW, Suite 500
Washington, DC 20036
(202) 232-4677
Write for *Turn Aluminum Cans into Cash* and other pamphlets about recycling cans.

Earth Communications Office
P.O. Box 36M39, #207
Los Angeles, CA 90036
(213) 932-7968

Environmental Protection Agency (EPA)
Office of Communications and Public Affairs
401 M St. SW, PM211B
Washington, DC 20460
(202) 382-2080

Write for pamphlets on recycling at home and at school. *The Recoverable Resource Audit Handbook* will help you set up a school recycling program.

Inform
381 Park Ave. South
New York, NY 10016
(212) 689-4040

Institute of Scrap Recycling Industries, Inc.
1627 K St. NW
Washington, DC 20006
(202) 466-4050
They publish a free magazine about recycling called *Phoenix Quarterly*.

Recycle America
Waste Management, Inc.
3003 Butterfield Rd.
Oak Brook, IL 60521
(708) 572-8800
Write to them for information on recycling in cities and towns.

Reynolds Metal Co.
P.O. Box 27003
Richmond, VA 23261
(800) 228-2525 for information on the Reynolds Recycling Center nearest you.

Steel Can Recycling Institute
Foster Plaza
680 Anderson Dr.
Pittsburgh, PA 15220
(412) 922-2772

Further Reading

Other *How on Earth* books published by The Millbrook Press:

How on Earth Do We Recycle Glass? by Joanna Randolph Rott and Seli Groves.

How on Earth Do We Recycle Paper? by Helen Jill Fletcher and Seli Groves.

How on Earth Do We Recycle Plastic? by Janet Potter D'Amato with Laura Stephenson Carter.

Buy Now, Pay Later! Smart Shopping Counts by Thompson Yardley (Brookfield, CT: The Millbrook Press, 1992).

50 Simple Things Kids Can Do To Save the Earth by J. Jauna (Kansas City, MO: Andrews and McMeel, 1990).

A Kid's Guide to How to Save the Planet by Billy Goodman (New York: Avon Books, 1990).

Modern Metals by Andrew Langley (East Sussex, England: Wayland, 1980).

Out of the Fiery Furnace: The Impact of Metals on the History of Mankind by Robert Raymond (University Park and London: Pennsylvania State University Press, 1986).

Recycling Metal by Joy Palmer (New York, Franklin Watts, 1991).

Re-Uses: 2,133 Ways to Recycle and Reuse the Things You Ordinarily Throw Away by Carolyn Jabs (New York: Crown Publishers, 1982).

What a Load of Trash! Rescue Your Household Waste by Steve Skidmore (Brookfield, CT: The Millbrook Press, 1991).

INDEX

ABOUT THE AUTHORS

Rudy Kouhoupt, a free-lance writer and a designer of tools and engines, is a contributing editor for *The Home Shop Machinist* and *Live Steam* magazines and the author of *The Shop Wisdom of Rudy Kouhoupt*. During the past 25 years, his articles and designs have appeared in *Popular Science, Popular Mechanics*, and other magazines reaching a diverse group of readers. He has always recycled the metal objects found around his home and workshop, and he has designed exciting craft projects for this book that encourage young readers to use their imagination and creativity.

He lives in Bridgewater, New Jersey.

Donald B. Marti, Jr., a free-lance journalist specializing in popular science, has written articles on environmental issues for Indiana newspapers. He is a member of the American Association for the Advancement of Science.

He is currently studying and working in New York City.